LOST LAMB

~ God calls to those who are missing ~

by
Tim Deal

Foreword by Reverend Father Joachim Ssebwana

Front Cover – The vast night sky is dominated by a magnificent star that represents the presence of God. A shepherd and two of his lambs gaze in wonder at the star, with the glow of the holy city of Jerusalem in the distance. The third lamb is distracted by the things of life, ignores the beckoning star and will become lost; the lamb took his eyes off God.

Back Cover – The lost lamb is found and held in the arms of Jesus who went looking for him.

Cover art by Cy Hundley

ISBN: 979-8-9867509-3-4

✠

To

Ashley, Jasmine, Josiah, and Spencer

May God's grace always shine upon you!

✠

The Lord bless you and keep you!
The Lord let his face shine upon you
and be gracious to you!
The Lord look upon you kindly and
give you peace![1]

---

[1] *The New American Bible (Revised Edition)*, 2012, Numbers 6:24-26.

CONTENTS

FOREWORD

With faith and hope, Tim's prayer is for God to somehow use this book to bring at least one lamb back home. But what he has written is also an incredibly powerful resource for all who seek to grow and remain in a relationship with the loving Father.

Tim reminds us that we are loved, and constantly in the mind of the Father. We might be running away like Jonah, persecuting God and His Church like Saul, making a mess of ourselves like a lost son, denying the Lord like Peter, or insulting Him, like the thief next to Him on the cross. In all, this book reminds us that God's ultimate plan is for us to have a change of heart and cooperate with the plan He has for all of us—being safely Home with Him. Like the shepherd who never settles until all the lambs are home, so does God, until all His children are home. As long as there is still one lost out there, God is continually searching.

I hope that reading Tim's return to the fold will inspire many others to reflect on the lasting love of God, the patiently prompting voice of the Shepherd. May all that have a chance to read this book get in touch with the readiness of the shepherd to warm the lamb with a loving embrace, nurse the wounds and bruises from the brutal wilderness with his healing and forgiving love, and inspire living hope in the lamb through the gift of new beginnings.

Rev. Fr. Joachim Ssebwana
Priest of the Diocese of Kiyinda Mityana
(Uganda)

All royalties from this book go to support the children of Uganda.

With Gratitude

I find the words *Thank you* inadequate to describe the depth of gratitude I have for those who are guiding me on the most important journey of my life -- returning to God.

Many will remain nameless, as I simply have never met them, or I've forgotten their names, but I watched their actions and deeds and learned how to worship and honor God from them.

Those I owe the greatest gratitude:

- ✟ Father Kevin Novack
- ✟ Deacon Chris Peterson
- ✟ Father John Jatau
- ✟ Victoria Deal
- ✟ Elizabeth Deal
- ✟ Kathy Andrews
- ✟ Julie Romero

This book is dedicated to all of you.

Time to Come Home, My Lamb

The Parable of the Lost Sheep

Jesus asked, "What is your opinion? If a man has a hundred sheep and one of them goes astray, will he not leave the ninety-nine in the hills and go in search of the stray? And if he finds it, amen, I say to you, he rejoices more over it than over the ninety-nine that did not stray. In just the same way, it is not the will of your heavenly Father that one of these little ones be lost."[2]

I was born number eight of nine children; our parents Theresa and Robert were both U.S. Navy World War II veterans. We were raised in the Catholic faith in a long line of Catholic generations. When I was old enough, I became an altar boy, and I remember that experience fondly.

Since I was toward the tail-end of the family, my parents could afford to send me to Catholic school from first grade all the way through high school.

---

[2] *The New American Bible (Revised Edition)*, 2012, Matthew: 18:12-14.

When I moved away from home and was no longer under the watchful eyes of my parents, I started to neglect my Catholic upbringing and became lost. Today, I realize that it happened over time when the things of this world crowded out my relationship with God and living life as He wanted.

Although it's not pleasant to put into writing, I'd say that I became selfish, and even though I have always believed in God, I drifted away from Him. Sunday masses went by the wayside and prayers slowed to a mere trickle...to be said when I needed something from Him. How sad is that?

Sitting here, thinking back over those lost spiritual decades, it is hard for me to remember them with clarity. Ever since confronting a force far greater than I, 'telling' me to return to my faith; staring into the past is like looking into a bright light and then walking into a dark room, I cannot see. God is merciful.

The narrative that follows are things I learned, or relearned, as I made my way back to my faith and God.

It was around Easter time that I first felt something encouraging me to return to my faith. It was not a voice, a physical presence, or a sign in the sky, it was just a strong feeling. I, of course, tried to shrug it off, but it was persistent and would not be ignored.

Not being able to shake off the feeling, I found myself driving toward a church I had never visited, fearfully preparing for an encounter with a priest I had never met. I knew this was the first step on my journey back to God and I was nervous.

✠

Nine Months Later:..

I woke up from a dead sleep, my mind restless. Thoughts about the path I was on to better know God swirled around and I felt compelled to write them down. By this time in my journey, I had returned to weekly worship, embraced daily prayer, and started reading the Bible every night.

This book contains those thoughts from that night. I am sharing them with the other lost lambs out there in the hope that they are helpful. I told my sister Liz that if just one person is helped in their journey to return to God by reading this book, it would be a beautiful thing.

WE ARE CALLED TO ASK FOR GOD'S FORGIVENESS

> "Repent, therefore, and be converted, that your sins may be wiped away, and that the Lord may grant you times of refreshment..."[3]

I remember the drive to the church. I will never forget it. My heart raced and time slowed down. I wanted to avoid telling the priest my sins, I preferred burying them in a deep, dark hole, but it was not to be. I pulled into the deserted church parking lot, took a deep breath, and stepped out of the car. I noticed that my feet seemed heavier than usual as I neared the door, they did not want to go in either.

It can be a hard thing to confess your sins, but we are called to do it.

There is a well-known Israel king in the bible: King David, slayer of the Philistine giant, Goliath. He sinned against God, repented, and wrote a beautiful song that I find comforting. Perhaps you will also –

Have mercy on me, God, in accord with your merciful love;
in your abundant compassion blot out my transgressions.

---

[3] *The New American Bible (Revised Edition)*, 2012, Acts 3:19-20.

Thoroughly wash away my guilt:
And from my sins cleanse me.[4]

Even after my visit to the priest, I remained troubled. I had asked for God's forgiveness for my many sins, and I believed that he had forgiven me, but I was struggling to forgive myself. I talked to my sister Liz about it.

"Try to let it go," she said. "God has forgiven you."

"I know," I replied, "but it's like a heavy backpack. I put it down with my right hand and immediately pick it back up with my left."

She listened patiently, like she always does, and suggested I go talk to someone.

Great, I thought, not wanting to tell of my failures again. I wanted to forget, move on, but that was not going to happen. It took a few weeks to muster the courage to make an appointment to see Father Kevin, who I barely knew. I needed some spiritual guidance and I was hoping he could help me.

---

[4] *The New American Bible (Revised Edition)*, 2012, Psalm 51:3-4.

On the appointed day, I found myself sitting across from Father Kevin, and he asked me what was troubling me. That was all that it took. My throat shrank to the size of a drinking straw as if a boa constrictor had wrapped around it, and my eyes watered. I was not off to a good start. Telling my story took some time as I wrestled to get the words out without too many tears. I remember that he asked me, "Why are you crying?"

I somehow choked out an answer that caused Father to reach out for the Bible lying on the table. He flipped through it and said, "I want to read you something." I nodded in response, safer that way.

He began to read from the Prophet Isaiah…

> But now, thus says the Lord,
> who created you…,
> and formed you…
> Do not fear, for I have redeemed you;
> I have called you by name:
> You are mine...

> When I heard the words, "**You are Mine**," they took my breath away, God did not abandon me.

For I, the Lord, am your God
the Holy One of Israel, your savior
I give Egypt as ransom for you,
Ethiopia and Seba [two countries] in exchange for
you.

Because you are precious in my eyes
and honored, and I love you,
I give people in return for you
and nations in exchange for your life.
Fear not, for I am with you…[5, 6]

As I write this today, four months later, I can still feel the power of God's words through the prophet. Something changed for me that day when I walked out of the building and into the sunlight, I noticed that I had left my backpack behind, in the room where Father Kevin and I had met. I have read Isaiah 43, every night since; the words are like honey.[7]

---

[5] *The New American Bible (Revised Edition)*, Isaiah 43:1 and 43:3-5.
[6] Not the complete text of Isaiah 43.
[7] *The New American Bible (Revised Edition)*, 2012, Ezekiel 3:3.

AM I DOING GOD'S WILL?

> It is God's will for His followers to become more like Christ. He came to show us the way, but it can only happen as we submit every area of our lives to His authority...The idea of handing control over to someone else-even God-goes against the grain of our natures...[8]
>
> ~ Reverend Billy Graham ~

I had heard that we are to turn our lives over to God, but I had glossed over the details. I needed some clarification, so I decided I would call my sister Liz for some guidance. She is more versed in these things than I am.

✠

I pulled the house phone away from my ear and stared at the handset for a moment, not sure what I had heard coming out of it. It took a while for my brain to process what my sister had just said to me, "You have to turn your entire life over to God."

"You mean the whole thing?" I asked.

---

[8] https://billygraham.org/answer/how-can-we-know-what-gods-will-is/

"Yes," she replied.

"But I have plans," I told her.

Silence. She wasn't buying it.

I rushed to add, "But it's scary, I have no idea what God will ask of me."

As if dealing with a child, she said, "How about each day, after your morning prayers, you ask God: 'Is there anyone who I can help today?'"

Hmm, I thought. I could do that. Every 24-hours, I could renew turning my life over to God. That didn't seem too scary.

✠

It was a month later and I had finished morning prayers with my usual, "God please let me know who I might be able to help today."

Overnight, 14 inches of snow had fallen, and it was expected to dump more throughout the day. With only a few handful of homes in the valley, I did not expect God to take me up on my offer that day. I thought that I was on Easy Street. I told God I was available, confidently knowing He would not use me that day…or so I thought.

As I nursed a cup of coffee, my wife told me that an elderly neighbor had driven down to get his mail, but his car hadn't moved in almost 30 minutes. She was worried and wanted me to go and make sure he was okay. All I could think about was why would anyone go out in this weather?

Trudging through a hundred yards of knee-deep snow, I found my neighbor, his vehicle stuck in the snow. It would take an hour to pull him free, using my tractor. Wet and cold from crawling under his car and from the blowing snow, I drove the tractor home. As I moved up the driveway, I could not help but smile. God had taken me up on my offer to help someone on a day I was not expecting it, and I was glad he did…it made my day!

Now, I need to get serious and surrender my life over to God, my 24-hour stunt is not going to cut it. Still a little scary, but as I think about it, God has always taken care of me.

> Like obedient children, do not act in compliance with the desires of your former ignorance but, as he who called you is holy, be holy yourselves in every aspect of your lives.[9]

I think my skull must be thicker than most, as it took many decades to realize that our family Bible was not a paperweight. I now read it every night, and sitting right there, in plain sight on its pages are God's words telling us how to live our lives. Some of the words may leave you a little confused, but there are many people that can help you figure out what God is telling you. I have sisters, friends, priests, and deacons to help me.

God blessed Father Kevin with the gift of words, and he was using that gift as he slowly made his way to the center of the church. His words rained truth in the pews. He asked if anyone had ever said to us, "Are you from another planet?"

---

[9] *The New American Bible (Revised Edition)*, 2012, 1 Peter 1:14-15.

"If we are living our lives as God has asked us to do, we should be asked that question," he went on. "Christian values are not the values of the world, and, if you are living them, people will look at you differently."[10]

The Christian values taught in the Bible are often the opposite of worldly values:

✝ Kindness (the mercy of God) — Showing the love of Christ through our actions.

✝ Respect — Because we are made in the image of God, we should always treat others as we would wish to be treated.

✝ Humility — Putting others before yourself.

✝ Honesty — Being truthful and sincere.

✝ Generosity — Using your time, talent, and money to help others.

✝ Self-control — Denying or delaying your satisfaction.

✝ Forgiveness — Letting go of an injury. (emotional, physical)

---

[10] The words that Father Kevin delivered during this mass are paraphrased.

✝ Goodness — Doing what is right.

✝ Faithfulness — Being loyal to God, family, and keeping our word and promise.

✝ Love — Having unselfish concern for others.

As people watch you live your life, hopefully someone will ask, "Are you from another planet?" Best compliment ever!

> The LORD is near to all who call on Him, to all who call on Him in truth. He fulfills the desire of those who fear Him, He also hears their cry and saves them.[11]
>
> Ask, and it will be given to you; seek, and you will find; knock, and it will be opened to you.[12]

Looking back over the years, I can see the faces of friends who I once shared many laughs and fun experiences with, but the demands of life, time, and distance have taken their toll on those relationships, and now, most are only memories.

Recently at a Sunday mass, I was reminded of the most important relationship anyone can have, a relationship with God. Here is what Deacon Chris had to say as he gazed over the congregation, "You can't have a relationship with someone unless you talk to them. And the same goes for having a relationship with God."[13] As soon as the words left the Deacon's lips, I knew them to be true.

---

[11] *The New American Bible (Revised Edition)*, 2012, Psalm 145:18-19.
[12] *The New American Bible (Revised Edition)*, 2012, Matthew 7:7.
[13] Deacon Chris' words paraphrased.

I now make talking to God each day a part of my life. I go back and forth between saying a prayer, like *The Lord's Prayer*, or just sharing a thought about the day like, "Thank you God for this beautiful day."

I do remind myself to be humble, honest, and reverent in my communications with Him. He formed me and made me for His glory.[14] I never want to forget that.

Talking to God has many beautiful rewards. He will never betray a word you say, never gossip about your weaknesses, never abandon you, never ridicule you, and He will always love you.

So now I work on saying little prayers throughout the day. A very important one is a prayer of gratitude. It is a daily reminder of how fortunate I am, and I want God to know how much I appreciate all that He has given to me!

[14] Isaiah 43:7 (reworded).

MOVING FORWARD WITH GOD

> But you, Lord, are a compassionate and
> gracious God,
> Slow to anger, abounding in mercy and
> truth.
> Turn to me, be gracious to me;
> Give your strength to your servant...[15]

Sitting here, pecking at the keyboard, I am debating how to close this little book...it was not so long ago that the 'feeling' had visited me and patiently waited for my response. Those that know my story say it was the *Holy Spirit* guiding me to not neglect my soul and to live the life God wants for me. Looking back, I know they are right, and I thank God every day for watching over me.

As I move further from the place where I was, life gets more joyous. God provided a roadmap for us to follow in the wilderness, and He will not abandon us as we walk the trail of life that is stretched out before us. Gazing across the wilderness in front of me, I see beautiful vistas in the early morning light of each new day. This once-lost lamb is lost no more; I am back in the arms of my Shepherd, the Lord.

---

[15] *The New American Bible (Revised Edition)*, 2012, Psalm 86:15-16.

FOOTPRINTS IN THE SAND

One night I dreamed a dream…

I was walking along the beach with my Lord. Across the dark sky flashed scenes from my life. For each scene, I noticed two sets of footprints in the sand, one belonging to me and one to my Lord.

When the last scene of my life shot before me, I looked back at the footprints in the sand. There was only one set of footprints. I realized that this was at the lowest and saddest times of my life. This always bothered me, and I questioned the Lord about my dilemma.

"Lord, you said that once I decided to follow you,
You would walk with me all the way;
But I have noticed that during the
most troublesome times in my life,
There is only one set of footprints.
I don't understand why in times when I
needed you the most, you should leave me.

The Lord replied, "My precious, precious,
child. I love you, and I would never,
never leave you during your times of
trial and suffering…(see back cover)[16]

---

[16] There are several versions of this poem. Authorship unknown.